London Happening

Rich Hebron

London
Happening

Rich Hebron

Books by Rich Hebron

Homeless but Human
Primary Ponderings

Nuance & Notes Series

Chicago Clarity
Paris Beauty
New York Energy
Los Angeles Dreams
Miami Magic
Milwaukee Sensibility
Mexico City Merriness
London Happening

Written by Rich Hebron
Illustrated by Kenneth Ferguson

Milly Moves to the Farm
The Boy and the Rocketship

Rich Edition Classics

The Great Gatsby

Rich Hebron is an American author. He has lived half his life in Chicago and the other half on a farm in rural Wisconsin. He fuses these backgrounds together to draw inspiration and live a meaningful life in a world accelerated by the internet and digital technology. He hosts the Rich Conversations Podcast where he explores self-development and talks with friends in art and science fields.

Connect with Rich: @richhebron

For those who want to make life happen

Author's Note

My first near-death experience happened on the farm. An oil line blew on the tractor and became engulfed in flames. I jumped from it. My second near-death experience occurred four years afterwards. This time, three men pointed Uzi guns at my face, threatening to shoot me. Fortunately, it was just another reminder that life will end—all our lives. So how do we want ours to be?

After initially going fast, with the adrenaline from the encounter lasting months, I decided to stop. The difference between speed and velocity is that velocity is speed in a direction. Anyone can go fast—especially in circles. But it takes skill and something deeper to channel energy with purpose. Refining purpose requires restarting at the beginning. Be open and see what's happening. Pursue curiosity and, above all, patience.

My curiosity led me to hotel lobbies. I spent time visiting different ones in downtown Chicago and just sat, observed, and wrote notes, often sipping espresso or red wine. An appreciation for details developed. Gratitude followed. Every thing was there for a reason. Nothing was a coincidence. The creators of the spaces aimed to evoke particular emotions and feelings in people. They staged a vibe.

I learned that design affects our mind and influences our culture. The whole of something is the result of individual things. From a pencil to a house. From a shoe to our cities. From a light fixture to our lives. The story of our life is the result of every individual decision we make. The universe is the result of every individual atom.

Beauty is the result of those small, individual components. Love is understanding those small, individual components.

My passion and appreciation for detail expanded from hotel lobbies to virtually everything in life and in people. But something I especially had fun with was observing the designs on building facades. My favorites were those resembling nature. They possessed the character I aspire to be: dynamic, flexible, playful, and fruitful. Things that are alive are adaptable. Things that are dead are stiff, rigid, and brittle. Since human beings are part of nature, the same is true for people and their ideas and perspectives.

I encourage you to reflect on the follow questions:

- *Are current environments failing to design nuance?*
- *If design affects culture, what are the ramifications of prioritizing cheap and fast?*
- *Is a society that ignores patience a healthy one?*
- *If individuality is abandoned, is Love too?*

This is a series called *Nuance & Notes*.
This is a book of nuance of London with notes from my mind and observations in the world.

In 2023 I went on tour with music artists Hobo Johnson and Bonelang in London. I recorded five sold out shows in different venues across the city. The artwork in this book is from that experience. I'm grateful for the opportunity.

It's hard to think of a city more renowned and active than London. Its intellectual and industrious achievements have helped shape civilization. Few places contain such striking polarity and influence. It's both posh and punk. It's uppity and laid back. The imposing rigidity creates playful rebellion. The city, rich in pedigree, remains unapologetically scrappy. It's offbeat and cheeky. It's hip and edgy. London knows what's happening.

Shot on iPhone 13 Mini

It's happening here
We're happening here

Curiosity will take us
around the world and back

We know how to have fun

Focus more on the value of things
rather than the cost of things

Spend more time with people
who restore and elevate our energy

Explore the world of eclecticism

If feeling stuck,
follow curiosity

Some will climb up a fire escape
just to be with us

Become aware of moments
and their parlayed significance

An open mind creates an open world

Full throttle or idle
No in-between
Maximize energy

Rich Hebron

There's a knowing of what's hip

A square is closed
A circle is open
A triangle reflects

We're intelligent, hip, curious, and significant

The world is here
The world is there

A place can have every thing
except great weather

Know what we like
Every thing is easier after that

Rich Hebron

Friends are great
See them and speak with them

Drink water
but don't make it our personality

Be interested and become interesting
Interesting is currency

Team up with the talented and flexible

While the world awaits our presence,
we're ruminating together on
our favorite artists and influences

Never feel sorry for our self
That's a bloody wicked habit

Rich Hebron

One's plain is another's curiosity

It's tragic that the young don't realize
their significance till they're old

Every small decision led to this
singular moment and its nuances

Get charged up baby

Have we become who we tried not to be?
Who do we want to be?
Design each action accordingly

We can only be our self
But we can borrow from others

Every one collects something
What do we collect?

We won't get far without friends

Something creates the opposite of its self

For every moment and vibe,
we can create a playlist

It feels good to love and receive love

We become our passion
or grow to be the opposite of our passion

A palm tree in the cold makes a statement

Navigate and move with shooting stars

Love our friends
and celebrate their journey

Let's go full throttle

A champion uplifts the collective

Live music has an energy
Magic happens in the moment

Few things are more fun
than playing with magic

Logistics can be such a drag
Partner with those who make it easy

Rich Hebron

Open our eyes
See and nod

Polarity generates distinctions

It's regal here
It's metal here

Amazing how our energy
is revitalized after true expression

Rich Hebron

Being original beats trendy

Curate and listen to dynamite playlists

Rich Hebron

The young set the tone

The world is at our fingertips
when we fear less

A crop top is a look and gets looks

Rumors thrive in dignified places

Brothers compete and inspire each other

Throw 'em back

No itinerary creates
the most interesting itinerary

Thoughts and ideas of the past
live in every step and breath

Rich Hebron

Polarity promises culture and conflict

When malfunctioning,
shut it off and turn it on again

Appreciate the old but lean into the new

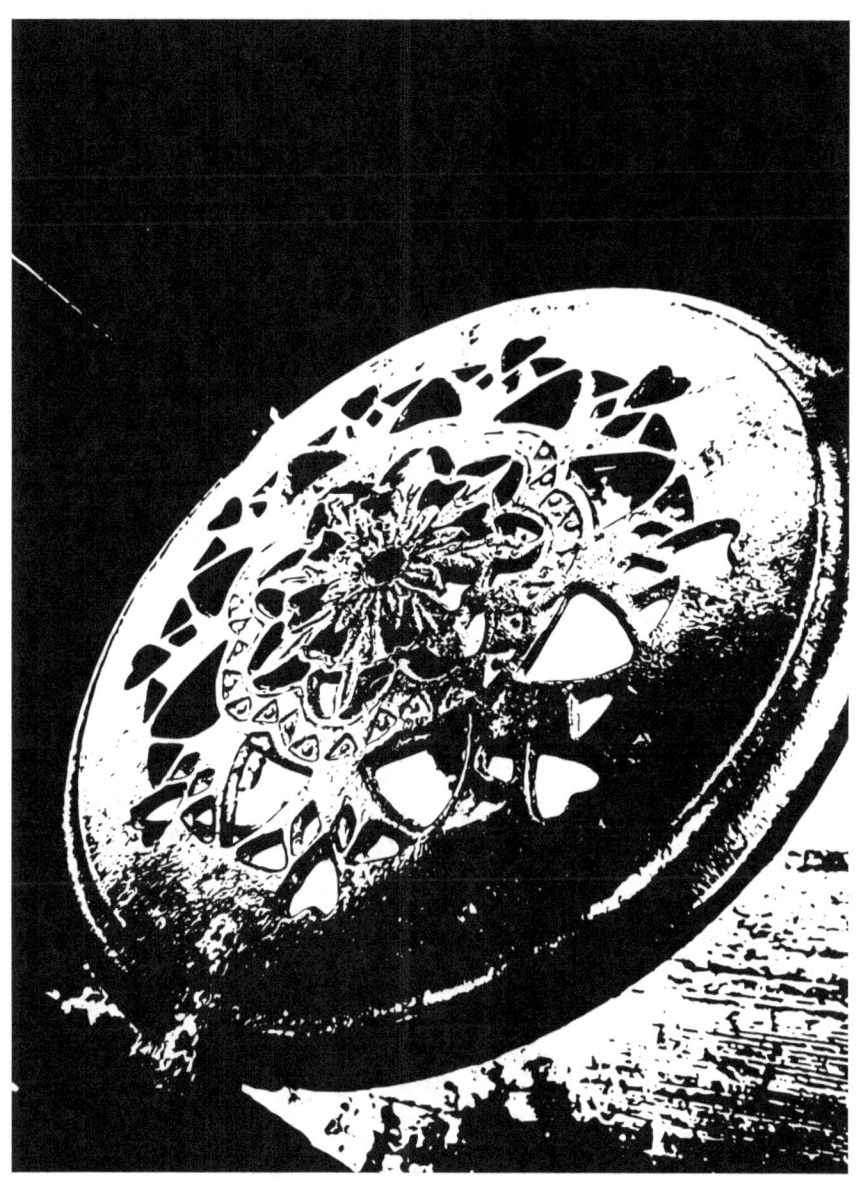

How can we collectively make our stamp
on the world and the story?

Each moment and each word spoken
contributes to the collective culture

London Happening

The world is inside
The world is outside

Rich Hebron

Without another being them
we wouldn't be us

The more dispersed the less progress

Rich Hebron

Get out and dance the night away

The world opens for the curious

Adjust the tie and smile

Grit makes beauty

Know what's up

Great things happened here
Great things are happening here
Great things will happen here

Talent occurs with belief, will, and practice

Cobblestone inspires
more than smooth pavement

Have a seat and observe the world

Less heavy, more light
Less serious, more fun

Never be too proud of the past
to let up on the future

Every now and then
ask if we're trying too hard
and if it's working

Listen to the moments of the old

When everyone is sitting, stand
When everyone is standing, sit

Let's appreciate this moment of time

Go for a walk and see where it leads us
and what information we learn

It's impactful to be both one and everyone

Be aware of when people
put thought into something

Rich Hebron

Step back and ask our self
if our actions
match the trajectory of our purpose

Add a plant to our space
A fake plant will do more than nothing

Rich Hebron

If each of us are more thought full,
our community will be elevated

Wacky people make the world more colorful

Don't worry
We'll be old before we know it

No need to be concerned with later
Be here now

Rich Hebron

Be useful
The world will find a place for us

Life and culture ebb and flow
but values remain consistent

Rich Hebron

We can look into one's eyes
and know the revelation to any curiosity

Every one can want something different,
but what does every one want universally?

Rich Hebron

We can relax and be our self with our brother

Where the biggest things happen,
the smallest things happen simultaneously

Rich Hebron

Time is nonexistent
when we are with our friends

Don't crave control so much
that we lose control

Rich Hebron

A cool current runs through the culture

Are queues attractive or repulsive?
Our answer reveals disposition

Rich Hebron

If we put our self out there,
there's someone it appeals to

We can be happy just vibing in a cafe

True talent deserves a nod and an applause

Feel the moment and dance

What new experiences await us?
Let's find out

Repeating the old is drab
Reinvent and reimagine

Explaining is exhausting
Cut back

It's good to be some where
with those who get us

Rich Hebron

Before we start anything,
let's take a deep breath

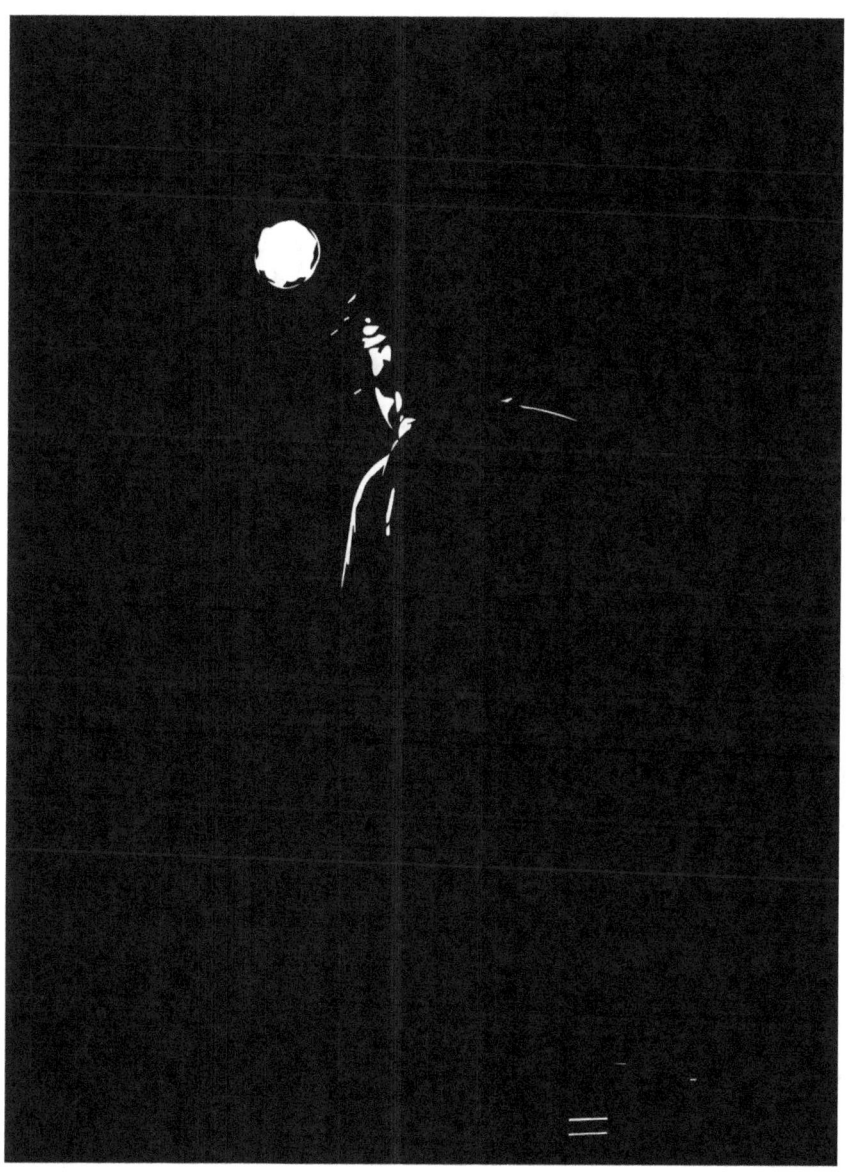

If we're flying high now,
what's our potential in love?

Don't be afraid
to have an unbelievably fun time

A place or person with no grit
has little character

Rich Hebron

History says the future
will romanticize the present

Feel and know the difference
between tired and relaxed

Rich Hebron

How we dress is an expression
What statement are we making?

When and in what setting
are we most in tune with our self?

Rich Hebron

Hang with the everyday and the special
for the greatest perspective

Be aware of battery life

Rich Hebron

Our periphery is useful

Talent gets taken care of

Use the past to visualize the future

Appreciate what is fleeting before it vanishes

Learn and build skills
Lead with curiosity

Don't stop now

Rich Hebron

Put a flower on it and blow a kiss

Have fun here and now

The most treasured memories
we create first involve people

Where we are now,
someone would love to start

A Thought on Cities

Our cities are our greatest invention. They're the engines of civilization. Cities are the hubs that bring people, ideas, and opportunities together. They generate energy and inspire the pursuit of dreams and a better life.

I feel humans are meant to be isolated in nature or surrounded by other humans. Fusing the two maximizes energy and accelerates regenerative processes. This is why I shuffle between living on a farm in rural America and traveling to big international cities.

Having lived in Chicago for over 15 years, I am an enthusiastic advocate for urban living. I believe that the healthier the city, the more dynamic the society and culture. I'm passionate about exploring and analyzing the facets of each city. I believe in competition and that our cities should be constantly learning, adapting, evolving, and growing to serve and increase the quality of life for its residents. I love observing and comparing cities, noting their strengths and weaknesses, the effects of local geography, the movements and flows, and how every small matter contributes to the larger matter.

Cities are where big things happen. I believed this as a little kid growing up on a farm and I know it now as an adult who has experienced their impact.

I'm proud to combine notes that can help realize individual human potential with artwork that demonstrates the beauty collaboration can produce.

Rich leads weekly self-reflection sessions to help people make life happen

Join in on the Rich Conversations Podcast or visit the Rich Hebron YouTube channel

Connect with Rich: @richhebron

Notes

Notes

Notes

Notes

www.ingramcontent.com/pod-product-compliance
Lightning Source LLC
Chambersburg PA
CBHW071758120626
46550CB00002B/832